I0866954

UNDERSTAN

Gavin Barrett

MAWENZI
HOUSE

©2020 Gavin Barrett

Except for purposes of review, no part of this book may be reproduced in any form without prior permission of the publisher.

We acknowledge the support of the Canada Council for the Arts for our publishing program. We also acknowledge support from the Government of Ontario through the Ontario Arts Council, and the support of the Government of Canada through the Canada Book Fund.

ONTARIO ARTS COUNCIL
CONSEIL DES ARTS DE L'ONTARIO
an Ontario government agency
un organisme du gouvernement de l'Ontario

Canada Council for the Arts
Conseil des arts du Canada

Canada

Cover design by Bhupesh Luther
Author photo credit: Richard Picton

Library and Archives Canada Cataloguing in Publication

Title: Understan / Gavin Barrett.
Names: Barrett, Gavin, 1967- author.
Description: Poems.
Identifiers: Canadiana (print) 20200250612 | Canadiana (ebook) 20200250671 | ISBN 9781774150146
(softcover) | ISBN 9781774150153 (HTML) | ISBN 9781774150160 (PDF)
Classification: LCC PS8603.A76835 U53 2020 | DDC C811/.6—dc23

Printed and bound in Canada by Coach House Printing

Mawenzi House Publishers Ltd.
39 Woburn Avenue (B)
Toronto, Ontario M5M 1K5
Canada
www.mawenzihouse.com

This is for you Leah, as always

CONTENTS

Understan *1*
To my daughters going to school *2*
What does a desert breed *3*
Flare, corona *4*
Never, always *5*
This fall *6*
How to die *7*
I could not leave you *9*
How we met *10*
Fifteen Aprils *12*
Humidity *13*
Two-blooded *14*
Third *15*
A dog has years *17*
The kiss *19*
Feeder *20*
Million's girl *21*
Novena to St. X *27*
Two buses *40*
The weal of birds *41*
Song of woe *42*
Gloria mundi *43*
When the whale: a conversation *44*
This way to the sangam *47*
Pickering *48*

Handy woman *50*
My friend the painter fights *51*
A wedding day *53*
Ten thousand thoughts on love *55*
Dream in a train, of a library *65*
Baga, Salcete *66*
Apologia *71*
Deccan *75*
Moonlight *76*
A fat woman's dignity *78*
Julietta, goodnight *79*
Portrait of Oudh *81*
Seeing Mary *82*
My father the sailor, in his 80s *83*

Thanks *87*
Acknowledgements *88*

Understan

Camels thread through the thorn trees.
They are insouciant grazers.
The wind stirs like memory.
Now I know I was remembering the future.
Stone shards bloom everywhere in this arid pasture.
Flowers of hurt. Bare feet fly, flail, blur, bleed.
Do you know what it is to die an honourable death
asked guides and priests,
monumental the question, the place.
I confess. I am my collected works.
Books on shelves, names like arrogance and tobacco.
Page upon unprinted page.
Blank and full, black and white.
And life? I ask as the women return with their brass pots.
Do I know?
We all fall silent. A fresco mocks us.
It shows a couple cavorting in the first-class compartment
of a train. We bare our teeth, voyeurs of the past
always looking over our shoulders,
wondering if we will be caught in flagrante delicto ourselves.
Long knives, short lives,
songs that bubble to their ends in pools of blood,
stories that started yesterday
and end four thousand years ago.
Once, upon, ever, after,
my children laugh, their pleasure plain
like prose, like poetry their pain.

To my daughters going to school

What have you made of me?
This air seems thin.
Do you leave with your bags filled,
sandwiches at the ready?
This is a summer of you in and out,
you, gone to camp, or camped in with books
and friends and ends of conversations
I snatch up as I come down the stairs.
The dog gone mad in a frenzied spin
searching for a summerlong ball. Look at your hair,
that cut suits you. I have spoken to you all year
all these years, but now you are full of feathers.
You're packed to go.
I have a camera ready in my mind.
In my mind I'm a better father than I am,
but you are always the same,
page girls with books read and written so many times
between you, bad television, reality shows,
sudden shining emotion, and something so much like the pain
of full love.
I made myself ready for the day but I am done with readiness.
Go, no, wait. Listen to me.
You are what you make of us.

What does a desert breed

What does a desert breed? I have seen stones, but not a reed
in the scraping breeze that sounds of sighs and needs.

It's not of dryness, this speech, but of distance and reach.
A marsh I know is a long wick of pitch and slime, soft suck and
stick.

When I fell from a ship, the seas in which soaked skin bled was
the measure of these,
slap, swell, and span, sounds, pressures, white powder pans—

salt has arms of wet hooped steel, cold flakes can drown a man
in a cargo hold.
Flats cut deep like knives, mirror-plate flash and always it is
light that ends lives.

Flare, corona

Your voice rises I notice
not noticing mine. We break
like waves or chips of flint.
The sun is closest to the earth
at the equator. Close out
the light in a squint
and shards of colour
kaleidoscope through eyes.
Imprism me.
Lash by lash, spectroanalyze
my what and who. Each blinding
flash of you may imprison me.
I realize in the lid-shut dark
my tide is in, this size
I have become may drown
you, this whip of light
you are may cut, burn me.
Flare, corona, be my crown.

Never, always

for Faith

You're always whirling in my songs and my mind,
always in my favour, never in my spite,
always turning in my poems, spinning in my lines—
never in my shadow, always in my light,
never storm, never cloud. Fight
and I see your eyes shine,
your words flash—you are always bright,
always with your brain, always with that spine,

always steady in your actions, wise in your young choices.
For years I bowed my head, listened as you sang those psalms,
loved most, and always, how distinct your voice is.
You are always in my heart, my ears, always in my arms.

A man makes his child and loves her, true,
but a blessed child made him father. That child is you.

This fall

Epithalamion

This book of ours, this red canoe times two, this boat of blades,
this heart of spades, this smiling door, this body breaking on
her shore, this drive in darkness, this railway station's sharp
elation, this waiting platform, this new form, this dissipating
this weight, this pain, this walk of thinking, this shrinking
sinking, this rising singing, this piping skirl, this girl, this
mother son, this father boy, this brother child, this baby toy,
this ancient love, this daughter joy, this island stock, this kiss,
this kirk, this lock, this vow, this now, this stand, this shock,
this stronglonghold, this fire escape, this leap from cold, this
stake, this shake of leaf, this lighted lake, this look, this eye, I,
aye, oh yes, oui, we, this us, this us, this is this this.

How to die

They say the best way to die is from the bitter cold.

I say the best way to die is living.
So many deaths to experience in every day
if death is what you love.

I saw a woman burn to death our blankets late to warm her.
That was a horrible way to die.

But she had died so many deaths
as she lived her way to that moment
a moment she had not set alight.
The angel of the lord is time
beating wings of fire.
She burned so quickly.

The best way to die is living.

Lovers dance with knives daily—their sharpest edge they bare
  to each other
so, sometimes, they die. A stupid way to die.

Romantic tragedy. Comedy.
The dull drama of a queen of diamonds
in sapphic swing with a queen of jade.

I saw a man drop a very large boulder on another man's head.
This death messed up my head.

He was dead, the man who dropped it but I cannot say how he
  died.
The man he killed died face first, asleep,
a thin sheet pulled over his eyes

shielding eyelids from the light
as he slept at the side of the road, the sheet
full of breath and hair and head.
But when the stone fell the sheet
was empty and silent and wet.

I could not leave you

I once carried that red gold sun
of the dust of bullock carts softclopping home
in the dusk. I had the sun.
It rose. Rose sun.
Sound of smoke rising
like whiskytalk.
But fire's
dull here, this is a dull lake of cold
soup and I am drowning in zero
in degrees.
Do not bring me your Indian
absolutes and nothings
when everything I loved has lost me.
There is nothing black in this grey.
There is nothing clear in this mash.
There is nothing white in this white.
Forgive me for leaving you
nothing of value.
I could not leave you.

How we met

Met her

hit her with the rock of my head
broke me

shook her hard water salt everywhere
sand in my hair

licked her with flames from my pages
burned me up turned gold

made her butter in my churn
slipped away singing my name

marked her with my teeth
made me unzip her

laid her table her cup
came for seconds

read her a picture book her wise eyes
charred my hull, sailed a boat of babies

drew her a glass of wine my blood
drained me the happy drunk

fought her she fought like a girl
left me bleeding and nearly alive

plucked her, my hair rose, felt flowers open
talked like the devil

rolled her into a joint into bed into a carpet
like Cleopatra queened me with her nose

smoked her, saw her in my mirror
her sawed half put us together again

crushed her heart, stopped the beating
bruised, juiced, drank me

met me.

Fifteen Aprils

You turned,
swimming.

Broke from the water
with your hair wet
your feet together

entered light and day,
you arrived
well timed
near midnight

a judge gave
your perfect dive
a ten.

You began loud
sang on the scale,
conducted me with your toes
caused an aspiration
of tired joy
and woke a poem
spoken
written on a sheet
of hospital paper
and finally lost into
air.

This was yesterday, fifteen Aprils ago.

Humidity

Grey fullsails. Judder. A plane.
A list of things of air?
The lake is dull,
pressed flat by crowds of shadows.
Bicycle wheel clicks the cicadas
past. Turboprop distortion. Flap
of sailcloth miniskirt.
Rubbersoled runners
creak and sigh and go.
The couple on the bench pretends to see
no one else.
Sweat gathering.
A congregation of weary faithful
saying their tear-salted novena.
Imagine everywhere ceiling fans strobe potlights.
Swans observe the boats drifting in before the storm
breaks. Cool gliders
in the heat.
It does not rain.

Two-blooded

for Nigel

Sideways I saw myself, threw a stone to my right.
The reflection rippled and walked out of sight.
My blood ran hot, argument in my veins.
I stabbed at myself, cut my wrists. No pains.
Later I saw you, covered in blood, still sanguine.
You broke bread with me, offered wine.
It was the first time that I knew
that I was cutting you.
I am the first of three. It means nothing to me.
I may as well be the last or the least or the last to be free.
I offer only one thing I know well.
I am under a spell.
Our mother cast it. Our father spelled it.
One could throw, one could write. Have you not felt it?
We are all a night of crying laughter.
The daftly brilliant becoming brilliantly dafter.
You are the sum of smiles, wiles, unhappy times.
I am your mirror image in older climes.
This is blood's thickness.
Thicker, than water, death, stupid sickness.
In the simplicity of density,
the surprise of intensity.

Third

for Russell

Shadow longer than my shadow
shade brighter than my sun.
Back then
no backbreak then
for us workers—
waker
of the father
I've become.
In our blackhairedbreed
the redder runner
from that rainsummer
the one
who was
no promised girl
but raising boy
the rising son
raison d'
dry. Stretched.
Sweet beyond my reason
dogfather
sonnabonnambulist
blue anorak
stroller borne you rolled and I strode.
Now you stride
as I float.
I have greyed to ash.

You are younger ember.
You will always be too young to remember
what
I saw said
forgot.

A dog has years

I see a man and a dog from my window.
The man is clog-shod, the dog shambling, happy, black,
wears a grey-bearded smile.
The man shines, the leash if on is tender-slack.

The dog is a fur full of panting summer
The man is a skin of wine and song.
In the warm days he strums and hums and plays.
The dog plays along.

I am told they are teachers, man and dog.
The man is a maker of adults.
The dog is a doctor of God.
Both are true, I have seen the happy mad results.

Some findings from their walks:
a list of the chewable properties of paper birch;
the comparative qualities of malt and motorcycles;
the idea that a family is a church,

that there are neighbourhoods of mind
and sugar bowl borrowings of thought;
invitations to dinner; forgotten books, words
of steady welcome, snowflakes caught

on tongues, the recipe for salt for winter;
ironies like a Shaker's love song, a dog's barked reasoning;
a story of Africa, the beat of a drum, the wake of a parent,
a pot of curry; that a strummed chord is a song's seasoning.

Those are a few. We have learned so much and now this:
the dog has gone. Those orange clogs are heavy-gaited.
Can a friend help a friend when a friend is lost?
We have new questions. We are sated

with answers. We are all owned by our gods and dogs,
orphaned by our parents' comings and goings,
caught onstage by our own floodlit secrets
in our self-portraits, naked at our own public showings.

This is pain this thorn-wrapped flower
this common knowledge.
This is joy, shared hurt, shared power,
this is love, all curve, all edge.

Make new lists friends.
This began as a poem of beginnings.
It will not end as a poem of ends.

The kiss

My father kissed my mother's face where we stood inside her
tomb,
a barrel-vaulted cradle space. Her name echoed in that room
and nothing was the same.

I spoke, said her name, read my piece and my father's mind,
my brothers sang love and peace. It was hard to find
and nothing was the same.

The walls of the grave were thick stone six feet deep.
We four were sick, the stone rang with grief.
Nothing was the same.

We hear of men. Have you heard a woman rise? From deep
inside her grave?
Women raise her high, thousands, from aisle into the nave.
The pews are flames and now nothing is the same.

Feeder

Whirlybird.
Shutterspeed flash and click
of beak on feeder.
The wasps stir the air
in yellow frenzy
at each approach.
This is aggression—a spin of
stinging, a dance of humming.
The whirl, the whirr.
Beak bent, neck stretched,
throat flashing red.
The hover, the wait, the dart.
The bird has it.
The nectar's in the song.
Is carried.

Million's girl

Contents

A song of Solomon of desperation c. 2001
The death of the spirit, the murder of intellect
The triumph of the material
The sung Mass of Corpus Christi
Ave Verum, Tantum Ergo
Million's girl
Money, her husband
Her daughter
The wrist-slitting of Million's girl for her daughter's attention
A ride in the Maid of the Mist
The advertising of Million's latest product
An evening of focus groups.
Including:
Dreams
Subway tokens
Telemarketers
Fragments of a movie screenplay

Prologue

Million speaks.
His voice is a traveller,
an immigrant to wisdom's shores.

> I didn't always live here in this
> jewelled city and he

spins. The camera whirs and whirls.
Million grimaces with the effort
but to the lens it's a smile.

From orphans' hearts come the desert
Of separations, the deserter, the husbandless daughter.

Million knows this.
The pain, his girl's,
the knife, his.

The dream of Money

Money turns in his sleep and hacks
and coughs.

Beautiful cars and fast women are the drink of men
who cannot find their way
to the north's shining lights and
mired in the unzipped codes, stay
in suburban pastoral nightmares,
culs de sac and telephone wires,
the cable trucks outside, on the driveway,
splitting the signal, always splitting the signal.

Money is phlegmatic.
Money has himself.

Million's girl

On the balcony of reason
stood Million's girl
waiting for love but love knew her not.

In the cellar the wines
sighed, a deep exhalation
rack upon rack.

This was love

When Million's girl married Money
he was not yet.
Just the compounding of his interest
played large upon her mind,
the size of his flattery—and they
loved the counterpoint of it all,
miscast half-caste,
fatherlessness that drew violin strings
across her nipples.
Orphaned Million frowned and nodded
knowing the bitter answer,
this was not Million yet
and not yet Money
but growing, even at a head shorter
growing all the while.
Lust too put in an appearance
as they turned in their dance.
At the wedding his obvious pleasure
was obvious.
So the music starts. Strauss begins it.
Then it turns and ends in a cage.

In her house

Million's girl has a house of rooms.
The rooms are filled with wall.

The floorboards shine with the zeal of wood
that has met the mop of a brown-skinned girl
who bends and sways with silent mind.
The pictures lean from the wall,
the fire hisses.

Money moves forward

Money makes things happen.
Money minds his business.
Money talks
to people, gets more than he wants,
starts with capital.
Money's credit rating is A.
Money drives a car that drives a sentence
full of vowels so Money buys
a consonant.
Money meets his clients and is impressed
with his own power, his expertise
in the face of their ignorance, his ease
in the face of their difficulties,
his appetite for their capital.
They rate a B. But Money knows
the smell of money. Stays fresh.
He assaults his female clients with
his aggression. Money's aggression is pure.
Money gives them gifts. Lust,
a meal of ambition in Money's own
loft and then Money
delivers. The coup de grâce
a fat joint—Money's not square.
Money hands them the thing.
A book. Money's well read.

A book. Money thinks.
A book. A book. A self-help book.
Who Moved My Cheese, Money intones
immovably. Or *Sun Tsu Takes On Enron*.
Money had not read these books
but gives them.
Money needs no help but
now. They know. Money smiles and things move forward.

Money bares his teeth

Money shook the shaggy dog off his shin bone.
No sex was worth this not even
glorious doggy-style fucking in the back lot
of his father-in-law's cottage with his
sister-in-law and he had done that
already. The dog was kicked off.
Money bared his lovely new teeth.
He had used them already on the
girl. Million's other daughter was
lovely now the way his wife had been
at twenty-one all full firm father's flesh.
Daddy's money made good teeth, good
teats, smooth-bellied beauty.
Money kicked the dog.

She could have died

On the day that Million's girl slit her wrists
open, Money was outdoors, jogging.
Money was barbequing a duck
grilling asparagus, charring fennel.

Money went for a swim, sat
in the jacuzzi, read a book, drank
a glass of Châteauneuf du Pape.
Money ran indoors when he heard her
scream at the sight of her own blood.
When Million's girl slit
her wrists Money was buying a girl
of twenty-one in a short pretty skirt and a halter
top and silly baseball hat,
in a bar a drink.
It was the first time Money had seen her
bleed. Not at childbirth
or during her period. Not once
had a knife slipped from her fingers
or paper cut her soft-fleshed
palms. She had never run with
scissors in all the time Money had
had her, that she'd been had by Money.
Servants did all that, even the bleeding.
Now Money observed the lines
she had drawn on her wrists,
the dark flush of red ink
thick with haemoglobin, slow, the seeping
held his eye his breath his anger he held
back, for now, observing dully
that this was blue blood then,
his first sight of it.
The wine seemed redder.
Money said fuck three times quietly
and with feeling, but all that was
later. First, Money was outdoors when
Million's girl sat on the stone bench in the bathroom
blood dripping to the marble floor.

Novena to St. X

a poem in 9 cycles

i. The church of the corner

Onyx holds a cup of ashes
a paisley, the ripened mango of my childhood,
hanging from the christmas tree.
Here in incongrous drifts of sand
white as snow, far from chinars now
bareboned in the acrid cordite air
of their beautiful valley
I haggle over the papier maché.
Somewhere a Ladakhi woman, her
skin cracked leather
must have chewed on this and
spat it out, newsprint staining her
lips black her
teeth missing gums aching
her hat felt
like it was winter. Planes land
in Leh, routinely they say
but routine is all that makes it so
in this high slow country
its dogs bred for lion-maned looks
and its dances with old cold evil
masks of spirit, and fat tea
salty with yak butter.

Or does some carpet-weaving
child do double time as the frame
stretches the field of silk

in knotted loops and satin pile, a tree, a leaf
a bird, woods, a garden where good
is brought by Allah's hand
while ink-stained lips move silently
like prayer moves?
Masticated, pulp flies into a bowl
kept for the purpose, is
mashed, pressed, formed, painted a repeating
field of star and crescent moon and sky or that
tree, leaf, bird, wooded place, garden of good
shellac hardening over it as eyes
glazed the boy knots his way through
the tapestry, sheen changing as the light
goes west.

The six men who live in the next flat
hiss and whistle, sunrise and sunset,
their fasts silent, their breakfasts loud
twice a day
all this far from home in a country where the locals
swear and drink not tea but coffee,
eat pork.

The church at the corner is famous for many things
pigs among them
a herd of swine that trip the unwary midnight
walker, catch bikers unawares.
Stories tell of pedals spinning in the gutter
cloven-footed chases in the dark
grunts and snuffles of the hounds of hell, eyes
not saucers but peas
breath rank from nightsoil detail.
A man dies once, from drink or from the pigs that
followed him home, the giddy wheeling

dance that began in the taverna
ended when his head hit the crumbling laterite step
hard and bled all over the red stone.
They find him there
dead in the morning.

This is a church famous for many things.
St Francis stood here and preached.
The people in the north were colder
or less tractable or richer.
The people here were certainly not more intelligent.
For a saint it was easy going, it must have been
it still is.

Let us talk of the crabs from the river Sal.
They have crosses on their backs,
the supposed work of that fire-tongued Francis
who traced the sign on one,
his first convert when none paid him any attention.
They multiplied. Cross-bearing crabs
scatter crossly across the muck
as feet approach.
This must be holy water. Hermit
crabs come out of their shells.
Fiddlers wave their lopsided claws and circle
through the slime
in a slow obscene foxtrot.

The parish of St Francis Xavier is not far from here.
A half hour by bullock cart,
twice that by foot.
Dugouts are made on the other bank.
Coconut tree trunks
fling off wedges of themselves

before the machete
and then flinch, withdraw and sulk as the torch
chars them, till light-hulled
from the licking flames they become themselves.
A boat is a charcoal log sliding
into the water like a snake.

* * *

On the low platform where the trees gather
at the lip of the fields,
scattered bushes hold molted snakeskins
like Tibetan prayer flags,
dry, unflappable, reptilian.
A herpetologist's altar.
The church glimmers across the dry sea
of sandy fields, white and blue.
A painted sky pushes it forward
like a ship,
a square-sailed caravel
in a huddle of lateen-masted dhows
a chapel, and other minor shrines.

ii. The church at the fork

Can a statue swim? The virgin at St Andrew's did,
upwards to the hilltop, porpoise-inspired, arm-locked
journey, foot-driven, breaking full wave
with ring of white, halo intact
a life ring thrown by God.
Ten generations of fishermen
come now to visit her. At home
another statue stands in the blue and gold altar,

gilt leaves wrap like serpents around
spiral columns—pillared dreams
woven by the dead soldiers
in the front pew, an advance guard of the dead.

iii. Cross Feast

There are four ways to the cross for the rosary.

Skirted girls sing veiled hymns.
They approach from the neighbour's land.

From east of the town, a rabble with knives and a grudge that has ached itself
into a tumour, they kill for graves and burial rights.

How many holy places can one heart hold?
They can be divided into the following.

Dying places made sacred by life leaving;
a holy room is a room full of last breaths.

Loving places. Loosely where one can be a child
or make a child. Breaths here race in shallow troughs,
bump over ruts, rise, in yells, or pleasure
muffled by the cupped hand.

Hiding places.

What is holy cannot be counted on.

iv. House holder

What Jesuit could craft this rare
redemption you brought me, a prayer

in a chapel that does not, will not
stop a moment and still,
moves not at all,
fixed for all
time in the firmament of your face,
in perpetual motion like stars and children
    and your hips ahead of me
    on the road to college in wet July
    my eyes riding the pilgrim whole of you.

Now thighs and breasts and I
and years and cups and plates and lengths of garden hose
pray along.

An entire house hums with you.

v. Painted church

Stained glass halves
scaffolding,
the cross crossed over
the gallows hung,
the altar steps forward,
the priest behind.
What we loosen
we find.

What leaves us grips us.
What we see trips us.

vi. Missa Brevis

Hymnals a flock

of white-winged birds
in their hands,
fat red-wine bellied.
Rows of them.
These things sweep the pews.
Eyes from the altar.
Sunlight, stained purple and red by glass.
Eyebrows singed a man
raised his voice in low assonance.
Swing low birds of prey
steal away.
The mass for the dead is done.
In the box is a scapular, a knife, an apple core.
Outside it is cold and the sun is bright.
Later, there are sandwiches.

vii. Jerome rings the angelus

When Jerome rang the angelus
the roused birds
flung themselves out of the bell tower
cawing their protest
at the clanging summons to prayer.
It was four in the morning
and not yet light.
They had nothing against the angelus.
It was just that they were accustomed to it
at the usual times: noon and seven pm.
But Jerome was drunk and it was all
the same to him,
wine, water, bread, body,
birds and the paraclete.
Later when the parish priest came down

to ask what the noise was all about
he found Jerome in a pew,
on the floor, cheek against
the cold marble slab of a dead Portuguese
major, and in the sacristy
another miracle. All the sacramental
wine had vanished.

viii. Of the angel

Of the old churches
there were saints, an archangel,
the mother of the mother of all gods,
the lady herself again and again
even Lucifer makes an appearance,
slipping in sideways through the cracks
laughing at the men of cloth
and men of clay and the bitter herbs of their sin,
but Gabriel's never picked for the team
when the sticks go left and right.

I am raising a church for this.
Let prayers be said for girls who rule,
pleas made for the birth of daughters.

I will burn pigeons and grass-fed cows.
There will be seven hills where the girls run riot
and all the captive boys cheer among the chariots.
Some prophesy and some sigh and look to the stars.

The smoke is the kitchen fire.
The charcoal and incense.
The smoke is food on the way.
Blessings.

Sows have sent their own tongues
for the flames.

Are all the prophets men?
Ah, men.

I will call this angel trans-
figured
gendered.
mitter.

The other archangel has its own novena
each Wednesday where the Parsi women
murmur the words in strong belief
next to their burqa'd sisters and veiled Goan aunties
share their fans, plump faces
pearled with sweat in the throng
as the buses screech and exhale outside.

The smoke is glory.
The smoke is not the musket's.
The smoke is not the massless neutrino's.

Gabriel in a glow,
of what,
scripture, fiction, a cure for shame.
a carriage full of grace and baby names for God.

How do angels grow wings?
Is there a consultation,
an eternity's psychiatric evaluation.
Are bird hormones strained
through the lace of
prayer veils
in metered doses?

This church I make
is built of apparition.
Air, breath,
messages like God's radio announcements.

A man was silenced.
That was a revelation.
A woman, then another, lifted.
Are these wings?
This is a man in linen who tells us the meaning of our dreams?
Who destroys to protect
like a gardener pruning?
Yes?
A book is dictated.
Three faiths fall
into uneasy brotherhood
struck by words like lightning
or rain.

Gabriel unmutes.

Amen.

This is worthy of rosary
monstrance, genuflection, angelus,
a church to embrace the pregnant bride
at the altar and those who speak to her,
hail, Mary.

ix. Jalpaiguri

It rains.

The jute fields fill with frogs giving thanks,

a din as loud and fervent
as wealthy Bengalis arguing
for some other brand of communism
in a Calcutta tea room,
cups clattering,
glasses misting as they bend to suck from saucer.
Other frogs sound their pleasure like guitar strings
plucked with such intensity they break.

Inside the cloister the sisters gather.
Outside, the last drunks eat their boiled eggs
over their last teaglasses of arrack
and as the prayed incantations
are drawn up by pitch-pipe drone,
toss insults and garbage
over the convent wall.
The wall has sickle-and-hammer graffiti
and the hand of the Congress party.
One holds, the others are held.
A metaphor for walls?

The nuns sing.

Their accents are varied.
What is the sound of rape in another language?
This is one reason some escape to this place.
Some are still midflight.
Brown birds in rough brown wool they now repair,
resting on this branch of labour
and the liturgy of the hours.
Their ears attend to the silence,
hear sanctuary.

The psalm is of sheep.

They remember their goats
in Coorg and Bastar
and understand with complete clarity.
The nuns pray for themselves,
for the busload of students
who ask their blessings for exams,
for the childless man, the sonless wife.
They understand husbandry,
grow cabbages by a carp pond.
The wall encloses pasture
for the most valuable thing they own,
a stud bull who comes to the prioress like a dog,
massive, steaming in the rain.

Ashram they call home,
work that is prayer that is work.

This is not easy.
It is like a bed of stone,
like their beds.

They pray for the obscene drunks,
for the muck-toed farmer turning his bullocks
in the slow suck of the flooded paddy field.
They pray for rain in the burning south
where their sisters ration water
even for tea, a southern leaf
from high blue hills with precipice-forests
wrapped in mist, bound
in filaments of stone-edged highway.

Their own tea is from well above the raincloud.
Darjeeling sits there,
halfway up the Himalayan sky,
and clicks her teeth in the fog.

Near enough to be heard over the fish ponds
with their milling rohu and climbing perch,
their glass surfaces now rain-hammered
into beaten copper at sunrise.

Eyes like the eyes of a slave
resting on the breath of her mistress,
to you I lift my eyes.

This is sung.
Then the boys and girls file out
in a hush of uncomprehending gratitude,
to the bus, to all the tests that lie ahead.

The sisters' devotion is complete.

When the bell rings,
they eat breakfast.

In the quiet,
memory consumes them.

Two buses

One: eight Nigerian women, high-headed taffeta,
white teeth going to a revival. Singing.

Two: twelve minstrel Sikhs. Beards twined to sidelocks.
A boy hating his reflection in the window.

The weal of birds

In the kingdom of the bird, wheeling about in air
describes a circle of exquisite doubt. Poets know this
and so imitate songs like raptors
casting about for an answer for a lark.

Song of woe

God of the hare-lipped pray for us
Lord of the circus freak
King of the tumourous
Master of those who
drown in bathtubs or riptides

God of cancer
God of pox
God of limbs scattered after the bomb blast

God of children who have choked
on airs of evil
children who have choked on
men, wool dust.

Gloria mundi

Sky full of windows
city of glass
earth deep with doors
city of grass
fire lit from fire
the full commonweal
dark inside pyre
city of steel.

When the whale: a conversation

How did your day begin?

Waiting for the morning bus,
garbage truck rattle shakes me from screen.
Fat-bellied sow style, muck stinkspittle
thread of garbage drool slavering out its arse end
sweet high perfume of rot, living things dying,
dead things crawling with life
the whiff knocks me back

to when the whale
came and lay dead on our shore
news brought first to nose
by that quick messenger. Stench.
Magnetic to vulture, crow, gull and boy.
We flow out to the rockstrewn bier
tide of intense curiosity
washing up against carcass ballooning
with ominously held mad-halitoxic breath.

Death smells.
The sweetness of putrefaction
a *bacilli at work* sign hanging in the air
shredding protein for minimum pay
fungal industry producing enormous cloud of flatulence
rancid blubber robs us of our own breath
but the pungency of hydrogen sulphide
comes over us like Hokusai had a nightmare
ingrate wave of terrible consequence
the eggs mother forgot
the acrid cat pissing everywhere and then dying,

a tone poem written for wind section alone.

An innocent couple come to fornicate
in the stunted mangroves is ambushed by
symphonic suppuration now in crescendo
and vomit their cheap Bombay sandwiches
cucumber tomato green chutney
he holds her hair off her forehead while the flood rises in his
gullet.

Was it a blue whale?

The whale is black.
Wet, sleek, gore pouring out the gash where the stray dogs
sit down to table without saying grace.
It is the black season.
The sky is black.
The thunderheads draw themselves up in the distance
and begin to roll in with the dread portentous certainty
of an Englishman declaring native lands discovered
or renaming a mountain for himself.
The rain, warm, slicks the whale.
Then the steam lifts lazily from the rocks
and the whale appears to move.
We scatter and watch the gulls take
our place, pocking the epidermis
like a mortar slab prepared for duty by
a flock of white *takiwallas*.
This damned corruption a Dharavi on its own,
stinking hive of labour and profit.
We retreat.
I hear—think—nothing of the explosion on the wind when it
comes
until the garbage truck today.

How do you feel about that?

A Portuguese caravel in full sail,
the swollen-stomached trash talker trundled away.
But next week it will deliver as always, the purest essence
of garbage on sidewalk,
a jus,
shining string of wet
my dog licks assiduously.
Later at home she will lick someone on the lips
dog that she is.

This way to the sangam

By the sea I met a man
out walking a holy elephant,
firm of foot
headed south.
Walking with him a length, we spoke.
Sounds fell from his mouth,
rounds of sand sank into the beach
beneath the animal's shuffling feet.

He confessed his journey was to the temple of the north
where even now a million men drew near
before the crowds arrived.
But he was going south I said.
He shrugged his nothing and read
my curious face, my foreign speech
considered his slow pace, this white beach.
Would he not be late?
But what good was any pilgrimage
if it ran straight?

Pickering

I stepped through the brush
my daughters and I and a dragonfly
sang and its faceted eye
spun, its wings a rush
and buzz of air and the reeds
by the creek at Petticoat Point
stiff-necked and bull-rushed, shook seeds
in podfuls to the ground, in a gust, to disappoint
barefoot girls who two by two tore down the path
in search of a woodrose, a thistle bush, a bathe
in the lake when the path wound down
like a lady in a star-spangled gown
on a spiral stair down past maples firs pines
down to the beach: standing in lines
seventeen giant cooling towers rose, a city
a fabled khan might have built, ruled without pity
dead men in the foundations
making them strong
with the stoic patience
of those who've been dead long
out there on the spit, in mist or steam
they stood serried as in a dream
at the foot of the bluff at the edge of the park
at the end of our walk
where the creek viscously slipped into lake
the city took me and shook me awake
the girls laughed unseeing and pulled me down to the water,
each hand in the grip of the hand of a daughter

panting as though I'd run, lost, a race
downwind, I caught my breath, trapped in my place
by towers of silence that hiss and mock
electric shock.

Handy woman

She was a carpenter
I helped
we heaved and pushed the beaming wood
sweated
zipper-sawed
tumbled up
to the bedstand at the top of the stairs.
We placed the wood and smacked it down
fore and aft, the beam stood
firm and the smooth
bare belly plank was stroked in place
all tongue and groove
ran a body's length to
the headboard.
She lay down and measured bed lengths with her body
and stuck my pencil behind her ear.

My friend the painter fights

A man paints, he paints his face, he goes to war, he flies
through space.
He throws a bright red ball into a stand of birch, calls his dog,
begins to search.

Below the bright lit blue of winter March, day will freeze, night
will parch.
Fly through these trees, fall through those leaves, spring
wounds and summer grieves.

Draw in blood, paint in stone, pain and art are bred in bone.
In boat of bone he floats, sails, his marrow is the shredded lace
of sails.

Machines light a nocturne's shades. Politicians promise graves
for all, and spades.
On the radio the news is grim, the world grows warm, minds
grow dim.

Eyes blur. Rain falls on the page and shapes poor prayers for a
gutted age.
Candles that showed our glowing tears and made our pleas, in
our golden years

stand in unlit regiments, pallid ghosts of light. This terror, this
second sight
drives us mad with the mundane fear. Fetish found and held
relic-near

the dark fills with sound. The surgeon heals with a wound.
The air is all wingbeat and hoof fall. The single paradox trips us
all.

The brush he holds may stain the sky with his bright-eyed
chemistry.
The red night is a trick of youth. Our memory is not the truth.

He sets his chin against the cold and refuses to do as told.
He picks a frame of cedar, admits in the end, he is a reader.

A man and knife are cutting close, the air grows dry, the
sandstorm blows.
In an art such cavernous echoes

We told such truths and lived such lies, laughed at the
exaggeration of our demise.
We lived such truths and told such lies, and every face was all
surprise.

He eats a plate of lentil soup, and sauerkraut and beans. He
knows what it means
to eat, to push away the empty plate, to rise the creaking
stairway to the room of means.

He paints his heart into a stand of trees, into the darkening
boughs, bees.
There is no shortage of sound, firestorms of flowers abound.

His friends the poets come to talk, fall silent. They walk.
In the park he hears the snow, they laugh at this together. They
know

that he must go, that he must stay, that he must go.
He draws himself into a cloud, and turns the music up loud.

A wedding day

So many ask the idea for the day.
A slip of a woman, a stout fellow.

A rental car, mothers in hats or scarves.
There are jolly laughers about.

A brother rolls in and a brother zooms in.
Brides rise in such pretty colours.

She is a vision.
He sees things.

I see my friend.
He is hiding from the well-wishers.

Many doubt themselves.
In its heart, in itself, a virtue

and a blight.
The beginning of illness.

I realize you can never give a woman away.
She is taken.

He is taken with her.
Such conjugations arise enormous.

The pen is full of meaning or ink.
We register everything in our catalogues,

intentions marked by vows,
vowels. I. You asked me to say this.

When we are empty we fill.
Will you have no more cake?

A scribbler arrives late, tired of the irony. The construction
that stopped him is progress.

Let me not admit impediments to marriages.
Or guilt to this pair, these gold rings.

True, the guests stand around the room like a Seurat
posed, a pixellation of good intent,

a poet on point like a setter, there must be Scotch in the room
or at least sacramental wine.

A brother perambulates.
I sit with him as with an archangel.

Elegant women use their hats as periods and exclamation marks.
Friends stir.

This cocktail is shaken and consumed.
Also, thrown into crowds.

The priest bemused speaks of his own marriages.
Bless you both.

Later, a mighty wind roars through the city. Tourists fling themselves
into the museum's new glass-sharded mouth.

Thunderclouds throwing noise and shadow in a display so biblical
it seems we are all on set. Lights. Action.

Another friend at the camera.

Ten thousand thoughts on love

This hymn is hers, he says.
That playful call is the start of days and years.

Inside our hearts lie knives.
Inside our knives are lies.

Closets are sexual things with their closing of doors and
 darkness.
So much is made of the passing of light and the closeness of
 bodies.

Our mind is the sun of a December day.
Our minds are the wings of a dead angel.

Kitchens are birthing rooms, this plate is love,
that child is my salt in your wound he said.

When we lie in bed, the flowers on the window sill
hold their breath and shake with desire.

When you take the ring off, the skin is naked
but still dressed in promises.

Make me no wreath of fears and I will climb no mountain.
She turned her face to the sun so he could kiss her.

Did you hear the neighbours last night? They were fighting.
I thought they were making love, he said.

She said spend me.
He said end me.

In tomorrow's paper he read of his demise.
His wife has said he was true to himself and so, to her.

The great truth is made with a complete knowledge of lies,
chisel to its marble block.

The Times spoke of war and bodies.
In our bed, we battle on.

Ten men in synchronicity celebrate
two opposites. Wedding choirs stand for reason.

Until. Undeath. Undo. Un-us. Un-part.
Vow, vow not to die.

Domus. Domicile.
Domesticated, your wildernesses.

The binding on your mind
is why you glide geisha-like. Is that a complaint, she asks.

Ghosts live. The living are ghosts.
These are our times. How can love thrive here?

Families are the burdens we carry into a marriage
like corpses carry clothes into the dirt.

In the nights when the lightning strikes
they hold each other, not from fear but hope.

The wind grew loud out of the northeast.
Only orphans understand its words.

The last thing you expect to be is a farmer growing wheat.
The last thing you expect to be is growing things.

So many letters. The proper addresses are lost.
Marriage puts the teeth into zip codes.

Shelflessness is a state. Beams, lashings, nails
can be used to build a wall, a bed.

Can they wait for each other? Waiting is a wasteland
for their insides.

They decided to explore the Nile together,
but only got as far as her source.

There are bodies in my room, flies in my soup
wingbeats in my brain. My back is an arc of pain.

Every other bite is searing, chilli on the fingertips.
Every other bite is a chocolate truffle filled with Scotch.

They gather in pairs on the beach
like animals disembarked after the flood.

She holds him close, he bends into a circle.
Supine they are raw code, a one and a zero.

Having clambered over many bare and rocky places
he trails his fingers over the dust of her face.

In Haifa, oranges glow in the dust.
Once a colour, now an explosion.

It strikes me, suspension bridges
are a guitar, plucked, cars clapping the flamenco

and plunging. The mist in skirts and ruffles.
God help those who vanish into love.

Canoes lie fat bellied on the beach.
His wife, pregnant, turns onto her back.

When I open my mouth, a frog of argument fills it, he said.
Stop, she said. No, you, he said.

They sat at the table to eat with their children
but became bitter as they drank with their parents.

He lay in the sand with her, passionate and then indolent.
Years later, they still found grit in their salad.

At the altar, three couples made the sign of the cross,
a mystery to themselves.

I paid you in children heavy like gold.
I paid you in gold, heavy like children.

I could not dance until I met you.
But you still cannot, she said, surprised, as he bent her over.

He had fucked her.
She had penetrated him.

That pain in our bellies is not the meal.
That is my child, she said. No, that is my heart, he said.

He cooked for her, fingers of asparagus, palm hearts,
a plate of marrow that he had sucked from the bone.

She called him because he did not call her.
She waited for him because he did not come.

She called him because he did not call her.
She called him because he could not hear.

She called him because he did not call her.
She called herself to hear his voice on their machine.

In the end, they were reduced to their magnificent beginning.
We were so young, so young.

The most beautiful thing about love ever written
is a lie about truth, and still a truth.

I am shallow. But still am thrust to your trough,
like breath before the end, like death before the grave.

Where Heloise and Abelard lie: iron-cast railing, true-love-
limestone,
tourists who rue love with old roses and bone.

On their anniversary she flew about, baked and laughed. He
smoked and stirred.
She serves cake now and talks to his ashes, a bird of words.

I have deep failings for you, he joked, explaining.
While he slept she choked him to death, laughed breathlessly.

At much-kissed tomb they did not kiss. At hands-clasped they
did not hold.
A raven's disdain. They captured it in a photograph.

I had a wife who exploded.
I have shrapnel in me.

He was fat, but thought like a thin man.
It excited her.

Sometimes it causes me to tremble. Some times.
At others I am rock.

A stoned poet is not a martyr. His words bend and hook to the
left.
Dear sir. She is pleased to make the necessary adjustments.

I fed the animal, she said, pleased. He growled,
sleep filling his lungs, like food.

Have you eaten yet?
It was the last thing she said.

It's fine
but I have a couple of corrections.

She sang but his ears were ringing.
He spoke and her mouth was full.

He sat on the porch mourning her. Breath hanging, he fell.
On a January night, he felt warmer slowly until the morning.

In the mornings, she hummed as she made coffee. When she read the paper
he watched her, watched what he could not touch.

A hard feeling to be your clock, to time all the talk.
Make me your watch, eyeing your pulse. Breathless.

I had shards and shapes,
she had drapes and shadows.

Curtains sometimes fall like axes.
Damn the bloody end. Damn the bloody start.

Arterial, this journey on central highway. A dotted line darkness.
Accidents happen, blood on the maps.

In salt pans acts of defiance. In jail, pails of nightsoil hope.
Independence is a movement, one of love's.

I gave her a pillow story every night, perfectly wrapped.
She always came when she unraveled the immaculate bow.

She hung a dreamcatcher over the bed and it filled quickly
with the men she had wanted. Oh, we ate well in those years.

Ever travellers, they ran out light and returned heavy
as camels of old with gold, spiced goods and stories for the cold.

Ever travellers, they ran out of light and returned heavy hearted
as camels, dry and old and cold even in the desert.

Childless, they sailed for all the oracles to make a child.
Were they true? Too early to say. The child is yet making them.

Jute is both cane and cloth. He watched his daughters sway
up the avenue of ashokas in the dusk between the harvest and
the hay.

He held her hand and turned off the camera to see the fireflies.
Now no one else will know.

What is dusk? Light held longer in a lake? The obscura of
smoke?
Cover, to slip a hand into a shirt or suck a fingertip?

I fought for you, he said. Fight for me.
I will fight you, she said, because I know you appreciate a fight.

Some thoughts are so vital.
Filigree of saliva, bubbles caught on a last breath.

Stun me. Stone me. Please phone me.
She threw the phone at him.

He sat down on the sidewalk. His voice shook, or the phone.
The divorce had begun. No dial tone.

Blood, infinitesimal infant of love.
The explosion of a drop falling into water,

will not killed could. Blood in the air,
in our plates, in our saucers, in the seat at the movie theatre.

Needle drums taut ink-pained flesh
and arrow pierces heart.

When the professionals measured the cup of their love
they spilled all their blood.

They fell down and instead of rising, began to dig.
It was a burial.

They lay beside each other not touching
on the naked floor until they were beside themselves.

Womban, wombie, wombly wombat
he teased her, my marsupial mate.

She punished him by holding his ear to her seashell belly
and swallowing him whole through the singularity of her navel.

My wife . . . I do not understand,
said the astrophysicist drunkenly—

she looked to the skies for help,
oh alien love.

Terrified of her own passion and its tumult
she took cover in the affection he gave in a fury.

It hurt him to admit he had lost.
Not her—them.

He thought the room was always the same.
But then she was always awake and he was always asleep.

They were such slight things when they began loving,
mere children. Now they are heavy and their slights cut.

Slash and turn. Slash and turn.
Primitive cultivation, harvest dance, occult sacrifice.

She said he killed them. But
they had lived so long after that he forgot to die.

She hit him because
he held her too hard.

She hit him because he assaulted her with volume,
volumes, tomes, times.

When she hit him
he cried, out.

She freed herself from him by refusing him.
She loved him mercilessly.

They had children who they loved,
who did not love them as much together as apart.

He slipped his hand into her warm, empty glove
to hold even her absence.

Their great battle was studied by friends
who thought they were at war but they were only making love.

He watched other men circle her with exquisite delay.
Her shoulders bared his teeth.

Obsessed with every button on her, he pushed and stroked and
    poked
and undid her. That was his undoing.

They fucked with books, spines
bending till they snapped apart.

The secondhand bookstore across the street from their hotel
    room
sold the story of their affair. As they were asleep, exhausted.

He read poetry to her until he was hard again.
She read poetry to him until he was soft again.

Salt wind, clove wind.
It scented her hair, curled her toes.

Salt and cloves,
they were salt and cloves.

She drank him and her throat was dry.
He consumed her and burned.

They travelled together and fell apart,
apart fell together.

They wrote. He could not spell.
It was bewitching.

Her writing rounded his corners,
edges, they crumbled.

Seven years at sea and one
wedding day in port.

Sailor, did you know she wore an anchor
like others wear a cross?

Acrobats in acrobat love they threw
themselves at each other and fell and flew.

Vows were said as the traffic growled. The bride raised
her skirt, his hands helping. They ran. Again they began.

In sight of each other, names were called and words were said.
That night they found themselves the same, one clothed, one
naked, one bed.

Dream in a train, of a library

Thoughts and taxicabs fly,
head rests against cold steel,
sunned mind turns to sky,
samples rest, simple rest.

Airconditioned magazine racks,
face on cool table, muted avocado whispers.
Opposite gigantic Zoroastrian figures, holy wood firestacks.
A cat eats a college, wipes its whiskers.

A rock shatters in a hundred strokes, brings new order
where kittens shred the weather into clouds.
The ninety-ninth stroke becomes a border,
nuns break habits, wear beige shrouds.

But light bends through reluctant lashes,
what once were visions are now flashes
of an evening's soft-lit sky—
as dreams begin, they die.

Baga, Salcete

India's summers, green-leaved,
season of the body's browning,
of mangoes in their season of ripeness.
and that moment of truth, the plucking.
The sweet rich passionate juice,
trickling down chin,
the last drop,
the final mango wisdom.

    And the final oyster and the last ice stick
    with its faded flavours,
    water sliding down the stick,
    gift of old hearts,
    weary coldness melting in the sun.

The same hot sun on the hand-hewn redstone porches.
Pungent smoke,
fragrant wood crackling faintly in the yellow fire,
a nervous flicker under the big black paddy pot,
overawed by the day's heat.

    Giant pot, cauldron of dreams,
    with an incongruous company of witches around it,
    Shakespeare under the palms,
    bubbling with its viscous sense of time.

No clock with steady neurotic tick could last here.
Timeless seamless sands growing outward,
mild-mannered desert,
outward to the higher land platform
with the neighbour's tree

(the stealing tree).

Branches of mangoes aswarm with ants,
and two vulture boys hovering below
for crumbs of ants
and guilt,
and the hope of scarlet embarrassment
when we were caught.

We ran away across the fields
to the pond beyond noon
where ageless black kunbi skins
tautly stretched over small breasts
as arms swung the wash down,
areolae noted—large, pink-grey—

with every swish and watery slap
of cloth on the slab,
fish darting from under dark rock,
startled by this sudden eclipse
of the slow solar minutes
of hot noon.

The red hill rose from there,
a hill like a wailing song,
as it rose, lifting up the longed-for
(to look at)
property,
red soil sloping up into the hot blue sky

carrying the fruit of knowledge
with their seed of secrets.
Strong spirits lived there,
mingling with the heady scent
of cashew, hung low on the trees,

whiffs of potent brew from the stills,

cashew juice running onto clothes,
and making fast a memory.
Mouths stained red with berries,
shout and twist in smiles
or grimace at some rare sour fruit,
strange on that sweet earth.

And always that red hill with the white cross atop it,
ringed by a low redstone wall
curved across the crest,
grass over it thickly, everywhere dry grass
a sluggish noon breeze parting it
to show the hand-hewn blocks,

the whole place smiling with gentle ghosts
even at noon.
Stretching out below, fields roll out,
an undulating patchwork,
cactus hedge and low walls
separating properties—

not ours to wander in
forbidden but irresistible,
unspeakably good for their fruit,
full of better juices,
suggestive of more succulent flesh.

We ran down with the breeze,
streamed down through the fruit groves
whistling past those songs of summer,
all gone culture,
all sadness
lost Portuguese,

handkerchieves flying in *mandos*,
the sadness of an ending
for that lost tribe of graceful bastards
the pale mestiços,
their songs humming in our ears
as we ran down like the wind,

past the muddy pool and its wallowing buffaloes
whisking away the flies,
chewing the brown water
streaming from their mouths,
white birds serene in the loud sun
foraging for mites in those huge
black cracked-mud-coated hides,

past the woman her breasts
hidden below the glassy water,
sunk onto her haunches,
feet planted in the silt
the pool's soft bed,
giving her body over
to the last cool place on the fields,

past them
over the sanded fallow fields,
up the loosely-earthed path
and higher still, almost to the platform,
when the wall of heat that had been built
by our quick feet in the sun,
stopped us, slid us
down the path, a tangled mound of slick limbs,
covered lightly in the sand flour.

We ran to the well, music of hollow
matka striking the cool green surface far below.

Clean, we made for nana's white-washed house,
beers that sank into our thirst
and drew poems of quenching.
Who can say God was not there
in the hot fat grains of boiled rice
and the steaming curry that soaked into it
with its island chunks of meat.
This was the bread we broke together,
this prayer we said.

Apologia

How petty honesties pervade lies.
Yesterday I read Paul—
if I know all truth
and do not care, I am noise.

But though much truth is given me,
I have begun to seek it out
when it hesitates, to help it on
selfward, rushing

where it glides, gentle truth, on muffled feet.
There is, yes, this eager fool in this man,
this clumsy heaviness
in pushing on a fuller life.

If this be loving less, he still does not love worse,
and the lack, it drops gently off.
Wilted, flowers pass, bring fruit to birth
(the poetry slackens now and then).

So let me cremate my soul,
burn it, for its bumbling entries.
Thrust into fire,
let it turn to ashes and return.

My cloddish wanderings are the earth
in which my learning grows.
I, it seems, must die each time,
for each time the pain

hurts you and kills me—
I am that moment blessed.

But you reel and I turn,
look, am struck again.

This could not be the grail
for which I have lingered in this frail bone.
The worm turned within the apple
and was bitten into.

It is the bitter organic taste
lying frankly on my tongue
and loosening my teeth.
True, mystics of a mundane kind

have sought me out and taught me all
they knew. When they passed,
I remained, obscure, circumspect,
a collection of anonymous graces

that vote (in specified equal voice)
at mealtimes and love-makings
for a general well-being,
a goodness of unspecificity,

an ambiguous glow.
There is after all, my sainthood
and my prophecies to consider,
an encyclopedic tongue and a vision.

A life worth not a song, not a line.

I pick my way along imagined grass banks,
along my mind's river, eddies and swirls
passing me in a silent rush,
and on the other side,

across the street, jewelled windows.
An entire city glitters vacuously at me.
The other side—
where people live their minute's worth.

Whores sit outside the university.
They eat bananas and squat invitingly,
their legs spread, shadows and echoes between—
their eyes are pits, with glimmers of more darkness.

Here the daily men and women descend
from inverse abysses,
from their pits, after a day of baiting.
Their scent is rank and bloody,

there is carnality and blood-lust
in their minds. But in steel compartments
they stick closely, unaware
of the sweat and smell and sex of the next.

Nothing works or even seems to
and the buses run late.
Back over on this side, where I live,
I keep losing my reasons,

my sight has, to my eyes, unknown purpose,
my vision becomes a variable, unquantified.
The vacuum never speaks.
I fall, falter.

A million other eyes stare at the ceiling,
embarrassed or angry.
Still I remain, to the last, a heroic growth,
a thing of strange conviction, vision-driven.

But still I fail.
I will beg pardon, retreat, find a cave for penance,
where I'll lie in rotting furs and dankness,
and light prayers and candles.

Deccan

Wise man, who first said hell was hot—
he must have come from this dry forsaken country,
this landscape of black stone
and sharp volcanic rubble,

this place of the dead.
Here the air is only rarely touched with life.
When it stirs, we shiver.
Cold sweat collects in a sticky pool at the base of the spine

like some clammy hand, lewdly caressing
those intimate inner planes of skin
where back meets buttock,
the cold touch of an old ghost scared by the heat of the
afternoon.

And everywhere, ash and stone and dead wood and bone.

Above, a kite-hawk circles,
vulgar life blessed by what strange wind
on this still afternoon,
the devil alone knows,

but he will not tell, we have not been long enough in hell.

Moonlight

There are places I remember
when my mind was young, doors that opened,
words that flew, a time when smooth
whisky flowed. It was a time beyond my eyes,

And tastes varied as they poured upon my tongue.
I was a supplicant, mouth gaping heavenwards.
For my pain and torn knees
I received good honey and a token capacity for speech.

Today metal elevators lift and lower me,
where I sell my goods.
(A bargain basement for the buyer
but for the seller, hell discerned on the fifteenth floor.)

Still, see, there are people to meet,
and met, to haggle with for ink and paper.
Yet even the working words I use, the statues
and idols I make, moulded clay-trapped gods,

could earn value, if all said could be done,
worth it for all that,
all that bowing and that scratching pen
hurrying even when only delivering dying words, dead lines.

If all said could be done, there are places,
times I know, when I would have loved to change,
loved to change this sky—throw in a moon,
an owl screeching doom

to the froth on the dance floor,
dripping jewellery as they sip champagne,

and nibble. Under their lace, wet lips shine with distant
glimmers of good intent beneath this moon,

and all the while my owl screams wild-eyed
from the woods and others abroad in this shadow
in fields straight beneath the moon, on hay floors,
sweat and gasp, tear clothes, bite

and biting bring warm heavy breath to nipples.
They catch fire. Driving hard below that great moon,
white circle, and in a haystack,
mice blessing their union,

their copulation and life, is all complete, consummated.
Away in the halls of grander houses, in softer beds,
others meet frustratedly, their sex is polite,
their minds neat, motives forgotten,

they always part as friends.
No struggle in the street,
no savage blood on bed,
some choose to let go of it all, only to die.

I might have loved to change,
this time, that place, but I have loved people
and blessings have found me
when I was alone or asleep and bound me.

(That is my excuse.) All said and done, I am amazed
how my life begins and ends constantly,
chances lost like words out of my mouth,
and all around, everybody, everybody dying or loving, quite
  without my help.

A fat woman's dignity

She moves through the café
brushing chairs aside like flies.
From underneath her widebrimmed hat
a surprise; behind huge dark glasses, the straightest clearest eyes.

A chair creaks under her.
Her weight is a disguise,
her girth conceals her humour,
surefooted she, a dancer hides within those folds of flesh, a pas de deux of grace and size.

A man passes in a blur, a man falls to the floor.
Smiling at her victims, oblivious to lies,
she forces truth out of them to their delight.
They laugh, they love, they sing, they dance—with her time flies.

Strange dignity in her smile. Sons
have fed at her breasts, her milk satisfies.
In her body
a woman's heart; strange dignity in her eyes.

Julietta, goodnight

What I knew of you last was much less than I'd ever known,
the years showed me still less of you.
And you shrank from us, flesh hanging on your bone,
skin in curtainfoldfalls from your flesh,
everytime I returned, less and less.

You'd snort and turn in sleep and hawk and clear and spit
falling into the dark would raise brittle wrist, wave goodnight
goodnight, a dewlapped arm nodding in agreement and sleep.

And I remember other nights of stars, the leather of your skin
in plastic sandals taking in your stride the sand of fields
lying fallow too long, kicking dust and shadows,
as ghostly pigs and swineherds dart for cover
in a soupwarm summer night with a breeze too thin
for relief or pleasure.

At the cross the rosary said, the candles guttering out on their
    own
wax-weaned prayers long gone,
just despairs waning now at wick's end, wordless:
babies wanted but unobtainable,
men gone soft, so steeped in drink,
too soft for any good but saving;
a dead love agonizingly near,
like a figure approaching in heavy rain but never making it.

I knew a place where a widow, a woman of property might
    stand
and piss on a tree at the boundary of her land
markings for others

a border of urine rivulets and the finest coconut palms.

(When it rains at a funeral in Goa,
curl your tongue around your lip and sip the clear drops
gathering
—not sweet fat rain, no, not these.
These taste of salt, tears, sea, sand, fresh fish fried in a pan on a
wood-fire.)

At home, you'd snort and turn and hawk and spit,
falling into the dark would raise brittle wrist, wave goodnight
goodnight, dewlapped arm nodding in agreement, sleep.
Goodnight.

Portrait of Oudh

The lady barks,
her grey dogs stir uneasily
and view the camera with some distaste,
only the first of many critics.

A face of line-drawing, a representation
of crumbling stone,
a squalor of diamonds, lost, servants gone,
palaces fallen.

She barks,
the great dogs' dewlaps shake,
the lady lives here.

This is a ruin.
In this overgrown gully
a mind easily wanders off the path.

The bearer who brings out a search party
finds no one.

Upon the dining table the last illusions lie,
a carpet of ancient glories spreads,
a goblet stands guard, cupping shades and shadows in its palm,
a pouch of diamonds by the plate,
crushed to crush the last mutineer.

A queen submits,
a resistance a reticence
or a lady barks,
great dogs padding softly after her,
tears forming in their eyes
noses wet with love.

Seeing Mary

Mary burned.
Mary turned and ran,
tongues of flame springing from her forehead.
Mary burned in May when
the earth is dry and dead.

He set a match to her,
licks of fire in the thatch of her hair
the cold and furious flame of the things he said
caught her nylon sari and it flared
where the cheap gold border met the red.

Mary ran across the field.
Mary screamed and fell.
A boy with a blanket smothered Mary's smoking head.
Burning hair has the whiff of hell
for those who live, but Mary is dead.

One brief night
Mary burned, a torch of kerosene
and bone and flesh, casting shadows off with violent light.
Cinders fell and died, and then Mary too, and lean
hungry barking dogs barked back the dark usual night.

My father the sailor, in his 80s

I see you as you are now,
broken-hulled, the bruising at your shoulder,
the Scotch in your hand asking for more,

while your teeth loosen into a smile.
Your beard is a cobweb of defiance,
stubborn bristles, or feathers for some kind of departure.

I remember you brought home
on each return the smell of an airplane cabin
when we opened your bags,

releasing chocolate, liquor, cigars,
and with these, in the folded shirts, the smell of you
along with a tin of cheese or a packet of biltong.

Your voice as much a recent arrival
as the cassettes of music I had asked for
and now played, every one of them.

Your awkward presence with its highlights of rage
must now replace letters that made us grateful
for their eloquence and grace.

It was distance then and distance now that binds us.
Like your father, a collector in the white man's
revenue system, you gathered and paid tax for experiences,

bags under the eyes for the mad drinking.
Ships turned back to port to deliver not cargo
but kidney stones and a flitty Fremantle nurse

who drove our mother mad as she drifted
in the sea of your absences. Did you know
she made me her anchor?

It nearly drowned me. A heavy burden for a child.
The day you came home I went to school in clothes
that shone like an angel, they were so clean, so new.

The day you came home I didn't go to school
because we had starved and were now feasting
and I needed to eat.

The day you came home you lost your temper,
your words, your distance, your wisdom.
I found your aftershave familiar.

It became mine before I began shaving.
The sting and spice reminded me who I was,
who you were to me.

I've re-read those evenings, when you held our heads
in your hands, blew smoke into our hair,
threw into our ears your odysseys,

mast-bound, cigar-thrusting, the oddest
fragmented narratives laced with enough reality
and drink to frighten big-eyed boys.

In the tadgola tree when the birds competed,
you explained the difference in their calls.
The crow pheasant's low drummed whoop-hoot,

the koel singing coo-ou. The green parrots'
mad chatter needed no translation, like the clattering rain
on the mangalore-tiled roof below our verandah.

In Dahanu, we caught fireflies for your matchbox.
They lit our way beneath the casuarina trees
along the beach, tiny cones under child-feet,

phosphorescent echoes from the water's edge
in the call and response of the night.
The cool sea licked at our bare toes like a family dog.

Always the salt about us. At the fisherman's cottage in Goa,
the beautiful moonshine stink of cashew feni
as we played snap in the blackening heat of May.

I remember the Lambretta,
two of us standing on the footboard
as we went to Soldier's Pond,

to swim in the shit-dark sea.
Where the stupid boys who hated us
wondered at our gills and fins

and envied your light skin
and our toys and our effortless departure
with the only father there,

our destination was ice cream
or a kheeri-kaleji stand or a thali
that we inhaled with utter certainty.

Now, before you fly I have to pierce you with a syringe
and meter a dose into the shrinking muscle
that you once flexed for our boyish pleasure.

I see you as you are now, tremors
that will be mine, your surprise
that your hip broke, that your sight

is a collection of shadows from your past,
that your shoulder and wrist disagree.
Your body behaves badly

like a random rickshaw driver at Bandra Station
who seems incapable of taking you
where you want to go.

You want to go for a swim.
For dinner with my girls.
For a walk in the safe dark

where no obstacles throw themselves
in your path and the paving is smooth
and unbuckled from the heaving monsoon earth,

where a man in his 80s with a decorated cane
that shines in the dark and day-glo laces
on his shoes may walk without hesitation.

You want to go home,
and you are home
and you have left home
and you are going home.

Thanks

I owe life and literature to my mother, Lorna, without whom I might never have written at all. She taught me to read and so to write, and was always my promoter, critic, and friend. I am grateful for the love of words I walk within, in the family that I went on to make with my wife Leah. Leah and my daughters Faith and April all read this manuscript and I am relieved they did not explode and are still here with me, loving as always. If they have any questions about me after all that reading, they are the same as my own about myself.

I come at least in broken bits from an Eastern tradition in which your guru grew you. Nissim Ezekiel praised me and published me and made me fear my own work less and love it more. Eunice D'Souza communicated with tobacco smoke and acerbic comment, her love for poets, and their brilliant stupidity. This is a good place to thank Ranjit Hoskoté, friend, poet, critic, and editor, who until now has published more of my poetry than anyone else and who continues to inspire me with his work. I remember with fondness and gratitude the late poet Robert Flanagan and painter Bob Anderson, both such a gentle joy in my life and who constantly exhorted me to get this work published.

I thank my artist-friend and collaborator, Bhupesh Luther, for the gift of his beautiful art for the cover of this book. I thank Mayank Bhatt, my too-modest partner in promoting diverse literature in Canada. When I complained that I had too many poems and had not the distance to fashion a book from them, Mayank pragmatically introduced me to the extraordinary editor and poet, Fraser Sutherland. Shukriya Mayank and doje Fraser for your directness and positivity. You were balm and incision.

Finally, I am deeply grateful for the work done by Nurjehan Aziz and MG Vassanji. Mr Vassanji published me for the first time in Canada when he accepted my poem “Apologia” for the *Toronto Review of Contemporary Writing Abroad*. Nurjehan and he are also the reason why my work was accepted for publication for the second time in Canada—this book. The work Mawenzi House does is immensely important and collections like this are proof of it.

Acknowledgements

“A fat woman’s dignity” and “Deccan” have been previously published in the Poetry Circle journal *Poiesis* (Winter 1993/ Summer 1994). “Deccan” was published in *Folio*, the literary monthly of *The Hindu* (January 2001). “Apologia” was published in the *Toronto Review of Contemporary Writing Abroad* edited by MG Vassanji. “Julietta, goodnight,” “A fat woman’s dignity,” “Deccan,” and “A Dream in a Train, of a Library” were all published in *Reasons For Belonging: Fourteen Contemporary Indian Poets*, edited by Ranjit Hoskoté, (Viking Penguin India 2002).